The Leopard Gecko Manual

FROM THE EXPERTS AT
ADVANCED VIVARIUM SYSTEMS®

By Philippe de Vosjoli with Roger Klingenberg, D.V.M., Ron Tremper, and Brian Viets, Ph.D.

THE HERPETOCULTURAL LIBRARY®
Advanced Vivarium Systems®
Irvine, California

D1040621

All photos by Philippe de Vosjoli except where otherwise indicated
Rachel Rice, *indexer*

Cover photo courtesy of Steve Cooper

The photographs in this book are courtesy of: Philippe de Vosjoli, pp. 5, 8–12, 15, 16, 19,
23 28, 37, 47, 56, 70, 75, 76, 78, 81, 84; Tom Weidner, pp. 3, 64; Paul Freed, p. 32; Isabelle
Francais, pp. 35; Bill Love, pp. 40, 41, 46, 50, 52, 54, 59, 80, 85, 87, 89; Ron Tremper, pp.
44, 60, 61, 67; Tim Rainwater, pp. 62, 65, 68, 83; Richard Bartlett, pp. 63, 66, 82; Kim
Harding, p. 79; John Tashjian, p. 86.

LCCN: 96-183295
ISBN: 1-882770-62-5

An Imprint of BowTie Press®
A Division of BowTie, Inc.
3 Burroughs
Irvine, CA 92618
www.avsbooks.com

We want to hear from you. What books would you like to see in the future? Please feel
free to write us with any comments on our AVS books.

Printed in Singapore
10 9 8 7 6

CONTENTS

ACKNOWLEDGMENTS

Brian Vietz, Ph.D.

My heartfelt thanks go out to my collaborators on these various projects: David Crews, Adam DiPrima, Michael Ewert, Deborah Flores, Richard Heidemann, Craig Nelson, Larry Talent, Alan Tousignant, Rick Williams, and Steve Wise. Larry and Rich deserve special mention as good friends and fellow lizard lovers. Larry is the authority on lizard keeping in academe, and Rich has been my right-hand man for the last five years.

INTRODUCTION

S ince the publication of my first book on leopard geckos in 1990, the herpetoculture of this species has undergone a revolution, transforming it into the first domesticated species of lizard. The leopard gecko is now the reptilian version of the parakeet or goldfish. Like the goldfish, selective breeding for xanthism (predominance of yellow and orange skin pigments produced by cells called xanthophores) launched the course for domestication. Today, at least ten varieties (morphs) of leopard geckos are commercially available, with many more on the horizon. As with fancy goldfish or koi carp, prize specimens are eagerly sought by breeders and fetch hundreds or even thousands of dollars.

Like other domesticated animals, the leopard gecko has certain characteristics that make it particularly suitable for this kind of endeavor. It is one of the hardiest of all lizard species, easy to keep, easy to breed, and potentially long-lived. It is a convenient size, neither too small to be appreciated and handled nor so large that it presents risks or requires enclosures that can't be readily integrated into the average household. And the leopard gecko is undeniably

beautiful, from the near velvet texture of its skin to its gold eyes and pastel shades of color. Like other animals developed as forms of living art, the leopard gecko has extremely variable color and pattern. These lizards also have nice personalities, by reptilian standards. By the time they are adults, many leopard geckos become quite docile and are slow and deliberate in their movements. The leopard gecko is one of the finest pets you could own.

Because of the rapid changes in leopard gecko herpetoculture in the last five years, it became clear that to write an up-to-date book on the subject I needed to seek the help and advice of other specialists. The quality of information gathered in this book would have not been possible without the coauthors: my good friend Roger Klingenberg, D.V.M., who has joined me on several writing ventures; Ron Tremper, a pioneer in the domestication of leopard geckos, who developed several of the popular designer morphs; and Brian Viets, Ph.D., an expert on the effects of temperature on sex determination and skin pigmentation in leopard geckos. In addition to the chapters each wrote, all three contributed to information throughout the book.

Many other specialist breeders, in an admirable spirit of cooperation and support, provided invaluable help, information, and photos. Special thanks to Bill Brant, David Nieves, Tim Rainwater, David Northcott, Bill Love, Richard Bartlett, Mark Leshock, Tom Weidner, and Sean McKeown.

CHAPTER 1

GENERAL INFORMATION

Leopard geckos belong to the family Eublepharidae, which includes all geckos with moveable eyelids. The members of the family Eublepharidae, also lack toe pads (subdigital setae—pads of tiny, hairlike scale projections on the undersides of the toes). Therefore, these lizards are not able to climb smooth, vertical surfaces.

The Eublepharidae family is divided in two subfamilies: Eublepharinae and Aeluroscalabotinae. The subfamily Eublepharinae includes all geckos with eyelids except one: the odd little Indonesian creature known as the cat gecko (*Aeluroscalabotes felinus*). The cat gecko is in its own separate subfamily, the Aeluroscalabotinae.

Some of the other well-known eublepharids (geckos with eyelids) in herpetoculture include the banded geckos (*Coleonyx* sp.) of the New World; Japanese and Hainan eyelid geckos (respectively *Goniurosaurus kuroiwae* and *G. lichtenfelderi*); the African fat-tailed gecko (*Hemitheconyx caudicinctus*), and the occasionally imported African clawed gecko (*Holodactylus africanus*). The cat gecko, a rare species from parts of Indonesia and Southeast Asia, is currently maintained and bred by only a handful of American hobbyists.

What's in a Name?

The scientific name of the leopard gecko is *Eublepharis macularius* (Etymology of the name: *Eu* = good, true; *blephar* = eyelid; *macularius* = spotted). In the pet trade, leopard geckos are also sometimes sold under the common name of Indian or Pakistani fat-tailed geckos. Some scientific literature also lists this species as the spotted fat-tailed gecko.

Distribution

The leopard gecko is found in Afghanistan, northwestern India, and Pakistan. The majority of the early captive stock was imported from Pakistan, although in recent years some imports are said to have originated in Afghanistan.

Sexing

There is only slight sexual dimorphism between males and females. Males are somewhat more heavy-bodied and have a slightly broader head and thicker neck than females. The only reliable method for determining sex is to look at the underside of these animals. Males have a V-shaped row of enlarged preanal pores in front of the vent (anus) that may exude a waxy secretion. Another obvious characteristic of mature males is the presence of paired hemipenal (male sex organs) swellings at the base of the tail. In contrast, females have preanal pits rather than enlarged pores and lack paired swellings at the base of the tail. Juveniles that are at least one month old can be sexed with some reliability by checking for developing preanal pores (in contrast to the barely hinted pits of female hatchlings). Use a 10x magnifying glass or pocket microscope.

Size

Adult leopard geckos can attain a maximum length just over 8 inches. Hatchlings have a total length of 3¼ to 3½ inches.

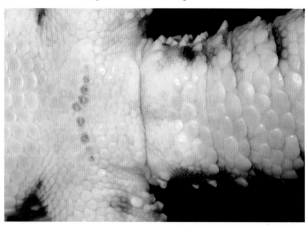

Close-up of a male leopard gecko showing enlarged pre-anal pores and hemipenal bulges.

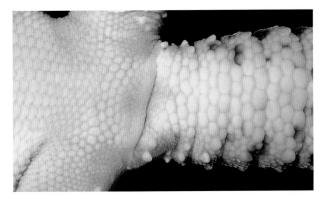

Growth Rate

Compared to large lizards, the relative growth rate of leopard geckos is minimal, a twenty-fold increase in weight from hatchling to adult. Hatchlings weigh 2½ to 3 grams. Adults typically weigh 45 to 60 grams but can attain a weight of 100 grams. Young adults can breed at 30 to 35 grams. Adult size is usually reached by about eighteen months.

Longevity

Leopard geckos are long-lived lizards. There is record of a male that was twenty-eight years old and still living at the Saint Louis Zoo. Herpetoculturist Ron Tremper reported another captive male specimen that was twenty-nine years of age and still living. Female leopard geckos are generally shorter lived than males. The current longevity record for a female leopard gecko is twenty-one years and ten months (Slavens and Slavens, 1997).

Other Leopard Geckos

All members of the genus *Eublepharis* are known as leopard geckos. Besides the common leopard gecko *(Eublepharis macularius)* of the pet trade, there are the Turkmenian leopard gecko *(E. turcmenicus)*, the East Indian leopard gecko *(E. hardwickii)*, the Iranian leopard gecko *(E. angramainyu)* (up to 6.8 inches snout-to-vent length [SVL]), and the recently described West Indian leopard gecko *(E. fuscus)*. The latter is of particular interest to hobbyists. It was initially described as a subspecies of the common leopard gecko *(E. macularius fuscus)* (Borner 1981) until Das elevated it to species status (Das 1997). The West Indian leopard gecko is one of the largest geckos, with an SVL of nearly 10 inches.

CHAPTER 2

THE LEOPARD GECKO AS A PET

Leopard geckos, even though they are the most easily kept of the lizards, are not necessarily the best lizard pets to be handled and interacted with frequently. They should be thought of as display lizards that will tolerate occasional handling. Still, leopard geckos seldom bite and, if they do, the bite is of little consequence. Also, after a little handling, leopard geckos don't scurry but instead move in a relatively slow and deliberate manner. As with all animals, the degree to which your leopard gecko is a pet depends on the animal's genetic propensity and the amount of interaction you invest in it. As a general rule, closely supervise children when they are handling leopard geckos. Animals that are regularly handled for short periods are usually calmer than animals that do not have such interaction. On the other hand, extensive and long-term handling is generally not recommended

With regular but brief periods of handling many adult leopard geckos will remain quite calm, particularly males. It is one of the qualities that make them an ideal pet lizard.

The leopard gecko is a beautiful species with some of the best qualities to be found in a reptile pet.

with leopard geckos because it causes the animals stress. Hatchlings and juveniles are smaller and more nervous than adults and should not be unnecessarily handled until they become subadults (5 inches long or so).

If you are looking for a lizard pet that can tolerate high levels of handling, better choices are Australian blue-tongued skinks *(Tiliqua scincoides)* and inland bearded dragons *(Pogona vitticeps)*.

CHAPTER 3

HOW TO SELECT A LEOPARD GECKO

Most of the leopard geckos sold in the trade are captive-bred juveniles, with subadults, retired breeders, and imports sporadically available.

Large adult leopard geckos such as this one may not be capable of producing eggs.

Wild Imports v. Captive Bred

Relatively few wild-collected leopard geckos are now imported into the United States and they are primarily of interest only to breeders who want to diversify their gene pools. Compared to the captive-bred leopard geckos offered in the pet trade, wild imported specimens typically appear dull-colored, beat up, and thin. Captive-bred and raised animals are best for aspiring leopard gecko owners because they are generally more attractive and healthier than wild forms.

Size

If your interest is captive breeding or having a long-lived pet, then the best choice is an immature leopard gecko under 6 inches long that you can reliably assume is under one year old. For beginners, animals at least 4 inches long are a better choice than small hatchlings, which tend to be more delicate. If you are attracted to a particularly large and robust adult, probably a retired breeder, remember that it may be old and, in the case of a female, probably not capable of producing many more eggs.

Sex

Both male and female leopard geckos make equally nice pets. If you plan to breed leopard geckos, remember that you need only one male per ten or even twenty females, and males cannot be housed together when mature. If you want to introduce a valuable new mutation such as albinism into your colony, a single male is a better investment than a single female. If your goal is to beat existing longevity records for the species, then a male is also a better choice.

Morphs/Varieties

There are now many varieties of leopard geckos and every year seems to bring some new variation. The primary

Representatives of lines developed by David Nieves. On top is a "tangerine" leopard gecko and on the bottom is a "high-contrast" leopard gecko with orange tint.

criterion for selecting a morph should be the aesthetic appeal it has for you. If your interest is primarily in the financial benefits of breeding one morph or another, then research your market carefully before investing.

Selecting a Potentially Healthy Leopard Gecko

The following are guidelines for selecting a potentially healthy leopard gecko. However, careful examination and selection prior to purchase does not always guarantee a healthy leopard gecko. Recognition of disease may also require veterinary methods, such as fecal exams. On two occasions I bought what appeared to be relatively healthy animals that were later diagnosed with coccidiosis (a parasitic infestation). On the bright side, many of the captive-bred leopard geckos sold in the pet trade are healthy.

Steps to Selecting a Leopard Gecko

1. The body outline should be smooth, the outline of the hip bones not visible, and the tail rounded—without wrinkles that give it a shrunken appearance. In the case of imports, a wrinkled tail may simply mean that a leopard gecko has not been fed for an extended period of time.

2. The mouth, when closed, should appear even, with no jutting upper or lower jaw.

3. Examine the digits (fingers and toes). They should appear even without swelling. No toes should be missing.

4. The eyes should be equal in size (see pictures in this book). Avoid leopard geckos with small eyes or with large bug-eyes.

5. If fecal matter is present in the enclosure, examine it for consistency. The feces of healthy leopard geckos are semiformed and somewhat pelleted in shape. They are dark with some whitish urates. Pale, light-colored, or yellow-orange feces, pasty feces that are patty shaped, and runny feces are all signs of possible disease.

6. Ask the seller to let you see the leopard gecko in which you are interested up close. It should appear bright-eyed

and alert when in your hand. Look at the belly area of the leopard gecko; the vent area should appear flush and clean without swelling, fecal smearing, or caked material.

Number of Animals

Leopard geckos, like many reptiles, do not require the company of cagemates to fare well. A single animal will thrive when kept by itself. If you want more than one leopard gecko, remember that adult males cannot be kept together or they will fight. Most of the animals sold in the pet trade are females, which can safely be kept together. If you want to breed leopard geckos, it is best to keep one male with several females. As a general rule, animals kept singly tend to maintain more weight and be more brightly colored than those kept in groups.

A container designed for rearing individual leopard geckos.

CHAPTER 4

HOUSING

Selecting an Enclosure

The most commonly sold reptile enclosures (vivaria) in the pet trade are all-glass tanks with screen tops. Less readily available are reptile enclosures with sliding glass fronts that provide easy access to the contents of the vivarium and facilitate maintenance. For display purposes, a standard 10-gallon (20 inches long) vivarium is adequate for a single leopard gecko. A standard 20-gallon vivarium (24 inches long) readily accommodates a pair or a trio (two females and one male).

Depending on space availability and the kind of design you want to incorporate into the vivarium, you may prefer a larger enclosure. Some large-scale breeders use plastic sweater-box type enclosures but these don't allow for viewing.

Although leopard geckos are not likely to climb out of all-glass aquaria without tops, a screened cover is recommended. It will allow you to safely place lights on top of the vivarium and prevent a leopard gecko from escaping by climbing onto vivarium landscape structures, such as

This is a basic shelter setup with shelter, calcium dish and a water container. The spotlight provides both light and heat.

plants, rocks, or wood. A screen cover will also keep out the household cat or dog, prevent the escape of insect prey, and reduce the temptation for small children to handle these animals excessively.

Substrates and Floor Covering

In the wild, leopard geckos can be found in rocky areas with clay-gravel soil covered by sand. In captivity, the first substrate choices of many breeders, particularly for baby leopard geckos, are newspaper or paper towels. These are inexpensive, relatively sterile, and easy to monitor and replace. However, many pet owners prefer to keep their animals on a substrate that is more natural looking and pleasing to the eye, and their preferred choice is fine-grade sand or a mix of sand and soil. Several kinds of sand (e.g., Repti Sand by Zoo Med and Jurassic Sand), including natural red sands, are now sold in the pet trade. Recently, a reptile-product company, T-Rex, came out with Calci-Sand, a calcium-carbonate sand that comes in several colors.

There have been some reports of leopard geckos, mostly babies, ingesting sand and dying of sand impaction. For this reason, many breeders recommend that babies initially be kept on paper and later, when they have reached a length of 6 inches, be switched over to sand. At the root of the impaction problem is the availability of calcium. Like many other terrestrial geckos, such as frog-eyed geckos (*Teratoscincus* sp.) and spider geckos (*Agamura* sp.), leopard geckos naturally ingest substrate matter as a source of calcium. Supplying calcium by coating the insects and offering dishes of calcium carbonate will usually satisfy their calcium needs and prevent or reduce the ingestion of large amounts of sand. The grade of sand is also a significant factor in impaction; fine sands are less likely to cause impaction than coarse ones. The kind of sand can also play a role, with hard silica sand more likely to cause impaction than softer limestone or calcium sands. To reduce sand ingestion when feeding, offer food insects in feeding dishes. Fine orchid bark, first rinsed in water to remove dust and then allowed to dry, has also been used successfully as a substrate. Sand/soil/orchid bark mixes and pea gravel also work well.

Shelters

Leopard geckos are nocturnal animals that usually avoid bright light and try to remain concealed from potential predators. A great deal of their time is spent out of sight and inside various forms of shelter, such as burrows or rock crevices. For this reason, it is essential to provide this species with some form of shelter. There are currently several kinds of commercially made reptile shelters, ranging from basic plastic boxes to molded concrete or plastic structures that resemble rock or bark and work well with leopard geckos. Many other landscape products currently sold in the trade, such as cork bark, dried woods, and rock, are ideal for creating natural looking shelters. Be extremely careful when using heavy materials such as rock or wood in creating shelters. They should be securely positioned with no risk of toppling, which could crush or injure a gecko. Use silicone glue to help anchor pieces together. Be particularly careful when lifting or removing rock or wood.

Heating for Display Enclosures

Like most reptiles in captivity, leopard geckos fare best in environments that provide a heat gradient, allowing for thermoregulatory behaviors. Cold-blooded animals like leopard geckos must have warmer and cooler areas within their enclosure in order to regulate their own temperature. The availability of a heat gradient in the leopard gecko enclosure leads to a better growth rate. If you own a relatively small number of leopard geckos (under ten), the following heating methods work well.

Reptile Heating Pads and Heat Tape

These heating media are available through stores that specialize in reptiles. The most common are subtank heating pads, which are placed under enclosures. If used properly, these are effective heating systems for leopard gecko vivaria lined with paper or with thin (1 inch or less) layers of substrate. Deep substrate layers several inches thick will act as insulation, preventing the heat from rising and causing it to build up to high levels at the bottom of the tank. Select a heating unit size that only covers 25 to 35 percent of the floor area. It is critical that most of the floor area be unheated to allow the animals to thermoregulate. To prevent mishaps, such as electrocution or overheating, follow manufacturer instructions carefully.

As a rule, glass bottoms should be slightly raised to allow for some airflow under the vivarium. If there is insufficient air flow in enclosures with recessed glass bottoms (most glass vivaria have recessed bottoms), heat can build up within the air space and cause the bottom of the tank to crack. Connect the heater to a thermostat to ensure it does not produce too much heat.

To prevent the bottom of glass enclosures from cracking due to over-heating, raise them above the floor surface by placing cardboard or wood along opposite sides. This will allow air flow that will prevent the buildup of heat under the recessed tank bottom. With large subtank heaters, use a thermostat.

Incandescent Bulbs

Some leopard gecko specialists choose to heat enclosures with incandescent bulbs in reflector-type fixtures that are placed on top of screen covers or anchored above open-top enclosures. Red bulbs can be used day and night. For most enclosures, a 40- or 60-watt bulb provides the desired heat range. To ensure this, use a thermometer to measure the temperature of the heated ground area closest to the bulb. The thermometer should read 84–88 degrees Fahrenheit. Incandescent fixtures are best used on vivaria that are at least 24 inches long with fully ventilated tops.

With smaller enclosures, there may not be enough surface area to create a temperature gradient that includes a cool area, so the risks of overheating are increased. Remember, the purpose of providing heat is to allow a lizard to thermoregulate by moving between a heat source and a cooler unheated area.

Hot Rocks

Although pet stores often recommend hot rock heating systems, some hot rock-type heaters are not appropriate for vivaria. The primary problem is with the surface temperature of hot rocks. Some simply get too hot (up to 105° F) and others have hot spots. All can lead to an unnatural temperature gradient, with a small hot surface (88–90° F) and the rest of the vivarium remaining too cool. This can lead to the animal receiving mild thermal burns and skin damage on the belly area because it must lie on a hot surface for extended periods of time to keep warm. With leopard geckos, hot rocks (the lower heat versions, not the hotter "desert" versions) should only be used as a secondary heat source. If you use hot rocks at all, place a thermometer on the surface of the heated area to ensure it is not too hot.

Safety

Every year there are fires caused by herpetoculture products, such as the spotlights in reflector-type fixtures or heating units, because pets topple lights, lights are placed too close to flammable materials, or heating units go haywire. Space heaters are a common cause of collection wipeout because the thermostat failed or was poorly adjusted. Think safety when keeping reptiles. Every possible scenario should be considered and the necessary adjustments made. No free wandering pets should be allowed in a room with incandescent heat bulbs or space heaters and children should be closely monitored around enclosures. As a rule, any room with heating and lighting products should have a smoke detector. Space heaters should be connected to backup thermostats. The more expensive digital thermometers have alarm features that can warn you if a temperature exceeds a particular setting. Helix Controls offers a thermostat system with alarm features, including a phone warning. Although the system is expensive, it could prove a lifesaver for large-scale commercial operations.

Relative Air Humidity

Like many desert geckos, leopard geckos do better with a moderate amount of relative air humidity in their shelter. Some studies (Nunan, 1987) have shown that relative air humidity inside the shelters or burrows of desert geckos can be high. Herpetoculturists specializing in geckos have confirmed the benefits of increasing air humidity within the shelters of ground-dwelling geckos. The primary goals are to reduce the rate of dehydration and to facilitate shedding. As a result, the overall health of the animal also benefits. If you live in an area with low relative humidity and are noticing shedding problems with your leopard geckos, you may want to take measures to provide a humidified shelter.

If you are using sand or orchid bark as a ground medium, simply wet the medium inside the shelter(s) once or twice a week to provide enough relative humidity for the well being of your lizards. Another practice is to use an oversized shelter with a small container holding a mixture of moistened sand and vermiculite (a common potting mix) placed in the center. Regularly monitor and water the container to maintain its moisture level. The above procedures are particularly beneficial for hatchlings and juveniles. The presence of asbestos has been detected in some vermiculite products, so breeders might consider wearing a mask when working with large amounts of vermiculite. Vermiculite producers have begun to regularly test their products, but if you are very concerned about the presence of asbestos, use perlite (perlite is a volcanic glass commonly used as a potting mix).

In dry regions, try using a small, plastic food-storage container with a hole cut out of the side as a humidified shelter. Line the bottom of the shelter with a substrate of foam sponge kept slightly moist. When using this kind of humidified shelter, always include an additional dry shelter in your setup. In most areas, leopard geckos will fare well without a humidified shelter.

Vivarium Maintenance

Leopard gecko vivaria are easily maintained because these are essentially clean animals that will defecate in a specific location of the vivarium. In addition, their stools are relatively dry and easy to scoop out. Scoop feces every two weeks and replace the ground medium as needed. Don't allow the vivarium or enclosure to get wet and be sure to provide adequate ventilation. Ammonia is produced when water is allowed to combine with the uric acid of the feces. If not removed, particularly in an unventilated, plastic sweater-box type of container, the ammonia can have harmful effects on the lizard's eyes, skin, and respiratory system. Excess moisture in unventilated enclosures can also lead to infections of the skin and digits. When leopard geckos are kept in sweater boxes in large numbers, all containers should be soaked in a chlorine solution at least twice a year.

Defecatorium and Defecatoria

The next time you play a word game with your friends, surprise them with the word *defecatorium*. This is the technical term recently used to describe regularly used defecation sites of lizards, such as leopard geckos. The plural of defecatorium is *defecatoria*. The leopard gecko is the best known of the lizards that use defecatoria and do not foul their homes.

CHAPTER 5

NATURALISTIC VIVARIUM DESIGN

The first time I ever saw a leopard gecko was in Paris, France, in 1962. It was kept in an 80-gallon planted community vivarium with African flat lizards (*Platysaurus* sp.), a giant day gecko (*Phelsuma* sp.), and a Brazilian monkey frog *(Phyllomedusa rohdei).* The leopard gecko lived in the dry half of the enclosure. I had the opportunity to observe the vivarium for several hours at a time, watching the behaviors of various lizards. This experience planted the seed for my interest in naturalistic vivarium design.

This naturalistic vivarium is ideal for leopard geckos.

A leopard gecko can fare well in an enclosure with a simple substrate, a shelter, and a shallow water container, but to observe a wider range of behaviors, purchase a larger enclosure and design a naturalistic vivarium. Given the opportunity, leopard geckos will display a greater range of activities in a more three-dimensional environment.

This chapter is designed to introduce the reader to this alternative method of keeping reptiles, which I believe is much more rewarding, interesting, and aesthetically pleasing than the utilitarian approach taken by most breeders. However, if naturalistic vivaria are not carefully planned and designed, they can offer a higher probability of risks leading to accidental injury or death than simple laboratory-type setups. For this reason, they are not recommended for housing valuable breeder animals. Careful attention to design can significantly reduce these risks.

Enclosures

The minimum sized enclosure for a naturalistic vivarium for leopard geckos is a 36-inch long vivarium with a screen top. Larger enclosures allow for even more interesting designs; my personal preference is a 48-inch vivarium. Avoid using thin glass enclosures because the bottom may fall out after landscape structures are introduced. Front opening enclosures, such as those manufactured by Vivarium Research Group, are best because they allow ease of access to inside areas. Plastic-sided enclosures with screen top openings (Neodesha Plastics or Vision Herpetological) also work well. Add a sand and soil blend consisting of two parts sand (decomposed granite, limestone, or calcium carbonate sand) and one part potting soil (I use Supersoil, a brand sold in large nurseries and home supply stores) to a height of 2 to 3 inches.

Landscaping

Add rocks and select dry wood sections to create natural-looking shelters and climbing areas. One problem with rocks is that a good-looking setup requires a lot of them. I once had a beautiful 80-gallon leopard gecko vivarium that fell apart when 230 pounds of rock and 120 pounds of substrate fell through the bottom. Luckily no animals were hurt, but it did teach me a lesson about landscaping desert vivaria. There are alternatives to using lots of rock or thick layers of substrate. One is to use broad sections of wood, which are much lighter than granite or limestone. I recommend cork bark slabs and neat sculptured sandblasted fig wood or grape wood, which are available in many reptile specialty stores. Combining wood with sections of cork bark gives a nice effect and makes it easy to create shelves and shelters. If using rock is important to you, you can make artificial rock landscaping by using polystyrene foam plastic as a core and then surrounding it with concrete. For more natural colors, concrete dyes can be added to the mix. An alternative is to mix concrete with soil or peat moss and to hand-form light rocklike structures.

I combine a few rocks with select pieces of wood, limiting the weight of the rock and wood to no more than the size of the vivarium (for example, 80 pounds for an 80-gallon vivarium). Because 1½ to 2 pounds per gallon of substrate is required for a decent layer, the total weight of landscape structures for an 80-gallon tank ranges up to 200 pounds. The landscaping should be distributed over a wide area so that the weight is not concentrated in the center.

Creating Landscape Structures

There are now a variety of commercially available products for landscaping reptile enclosures, ranging from cast plastic or concrete shelters to a wide selection of wood, bark, and rock. Various landscape structures can also be easily created using a concrete-based mix.

Form ground-level shelters and basking sites by overlapping flattened rocks or safer cork bark sections. Ramps that allow a gecko to climb from ground level to an elevated site can be made with sections of bark or thick wood. Rest the base on the ground and the end on the elevated shelter. With overhanging shelters, you can observe geckos sleeping during the day. Shelters with a broad overhang provide enough shade from overhead lights that leopard geckos will not mind resting under the overhang during the day.

Plants

For decorative purposes, plants can be added to a leopard gecko vivarium. Snake plants (*Sansevieria* sp.) come in a variety of shapes and sizes and can be introduced in broad shallow pots buried in the substrate or planted directly in a sand/soil substrate mix behind landscape structures. Small pony-tailed palms *(Beaucarnea recurvata)* with grasslike leaves also thrive in this kind of vivarium. Other choices include succulent philodendron *(Zamiaculcas zamiifolia* fares well in bright shade), haworthias *(Hathworthia)*, climbing aloe *(Aloe ciliaris)*, and caudexed figs *(Ficus petiolaris)*, which can be bought by mail order from cactus and succulent nurseries. One of the few cacti to work consistently well in vivaria is the padded and nearly spineless tree opuntia *(Consolea falcate)*. Good levels of daytime lighting (two to four fluorescent bulbs) are a must to keep these plants thriving.

Other Animals

In large vivaria, it is possible to keep other lizards with adult leopard geckos. I have successfully maintained pairs of collared lizards *(Crotaphytus* sp.) with these geckos. South African flat-lizards *(Platysaurus* sp.) and small girdle-tailed lizards *(Cordylus* sp.) can also be kept successfully with leopard geckos. The lizards in a combined vivarium should be approximately the same size and have different niche requirements (e.g., collared lizards are active during the day and leopard geckos at night). They should, however, come from habitats with similar climatic and geographic/topographic characteristics (e.g., desert/moderate relative humidity with daytime highs in the high 80s to low 90s F and night drops into the 70s F, with a combination of rock and sandy soil substrate).

All species should be quarantined and evaluated for disease prior to introduction into a community vivarium. Remember, little research has been done on successfully keeping species together, so keep a close eye on mixed vivaria. While some species will fare well together, others have to be removed when a problem is detected.

Lights and Heating

Use two full-spectrum fluorescent bulbs (e.g., Vita Lite) running the length of the enclosure for growing plants and general light quality. If diurnal (active during the daylight) basking lizards, such as collared lizards and armadillo lizards, are kept in the same vivarium, then use a high UV-B fluorescent reptile bulb (e.g., Reptisun 5.0 from Zoo Med or Reptile D- Light) as a substitute for one of the full-spectrum bulbs. In enclosures at least 48 inches long, place one or two spotlights over an area of stacked rock or wood to provide a basking area. If leopard geckos are kept alone, the basking area should be maintained at 85–90° F; if kept with diurnal friends, the basking area should be 90–95° F when measured at the area closest to the light. Keep the lights on for fourteen hours a day, except during two to three winter months when they should be reduced to ten hours a day to simulate a photoperiod reduction. At night, use one or two 25-watt red bulbs to provide mild heat and to allow observation of the lizards' nocturnal activity. A hot rock-type heater can be included as a secondary heat source. Use the lower heat range hot rocks rather than the higher heat "desert" type.

Maintenance

Lights should be on timers. The plants should be watered once or twice a week, as needed. To keep the vivarium attractive, wipe the glass sides clean once a week. Use a 50-percent solution of glass cleaner, such as Windex, on a paper towel, but be sure to wipe the sides dry. Do not mist the tank sides with cleaner; you don't want your animals to drink glass-cleaning solution from the sides of the vivarium. Check lights and timers regularly and place a thermometer in the vivarium.

CHAPTER 6

FEEDING

Leopard geckos typically feed on live, moving insect prey. Before the consistent availability of commercially raised crickets, many herpetoculturists successfully maintained their lizards for years on a diet consisting primarily of mealworms. However, breeding success was inconsistent and raising hatchlings was problematic until herpetoculturists started feeding insects that had been gut-loaded (fed a nutritional meal prior to offering) and dusted with a powdered vitamin/mineral mix.

Size of Prey

As a general rule, food items such as insects and so-called pink mice should be no more than the length, and less than half the width, of the lizard's head. Pink or pinkie mice are newborns that have not yet begun to grow fur. Older mice are often referred to as fuzzy mice.

Diet Selection

The best diet for leopard geckos consists of appropriately sized, commercially raised crickets and/or mealworms. As part of a varied adult diet, occasionally include pink mice, wax worms, and king mealworms in small amounts. King

mealworms are optional but are used by some breeders to fatten up animals. You should be careful not to overfeed with mealworms. Some large commercial breeders have been quite successful in maintaining their animals exclusively on mealworms that are raised on a high-quality diet and supplemented with a vitamin/mineral powder.

Other diets currently on the market include supplemented dried crickets and a frozen prepared diet. Leopard geckos usually need to be conditioned to feed on these non-moving diets. Some take to them, others don't.

Food Preparation

Prior to feeding your leopard gecko, gut-load your crickets and mealworms by placing them overnight in a plastic terrarium and offering a high quality diet. Commercial cricket diets, powdered rodent chow, Layena-brand chicken mash, baby cereal flakes, grated carrot sections, orange sections, and kale can all be used as part of a varied diet for insect prey.

Many breeders also add calcium carbonate or a calcium/vitamin D_3 supplement to the insect diet. As a source of water, offer crickets a slice of orange; provide mealworms slices of carrot. Grated squash and cooked yam can be used for variety.

Vitamin/Mineral Supplementation

While some lizards have narrow tolerance and requirement ranges for certain vitamins and minerals, leopard geckos are generally hardy and tolerate a wide range of supplementation regimens. This is fortunate because no methodical research has been published on the optimal supplementation formula for keeping and breeding most lizards, including leopard geckos. The one important requirement for leopard geckos is calcium, which should be supplied in the form of calcium carbonate or calcium gluconate. To ensure that enough calcium is available to leopard geckos, the standard practice is to keep a small container, such as a jar lid, of powdered calcium carbonate or gluconate in the vivarium at all times. Many breeders choose to use a calcium/vitamin D_3 supplement (Miner-all, Reptocal, Rep Cal, and T-Rex 2:1 are all fine) to ensure high egg production. It is important, however, to remember that the long-term effects of high levels of vitamin D_3 have not been determined in leopard geckos.

In addition to a dish of calcium, you can coat insects with a vitamin/mineral mix. The mix formulas vary greatly and there is little information on the long-term effects of various supplements, although some breeders suspect that excessive levels of vitamin D_3 and vitamin A may be associated with a high incidence of birth defects or "dead in the shell" rates. Some breeders primarily use calcium/D_3 supplements; others use a reptile multivitamin/mineral powder (a wide range of products is now available in the pet trade) combined with calcium carbonate. A mix that has performed well for many keepers consists of one part reptile or bird powdered multivitamin/mineral supplement with two parts powdered calcium carbonate or calcium gluconate. To coat insects with supplement, simply add a small amount of mix (a small pinch is all that is needed for one animal) into a feeding jar. Put the insects into the jar, gently swirl so they are lightly coated, then drop them into the vivarium feeding dish.

Immature leopard geckos can be supplemented at every feeding. Adults will fare well when supplemented only twice a week, although breeders often continue a high supplementation regime to ensure good egg production in females.

How and When to Feed

The best way to feed leopard geckos is to offer food insects in shallow ceramic dishes, glass ashtrays, plastic jars, or small, plastic pet dishes. This will prevent mealworms from escaping or burrowing into substrate and reduce the rate at which crickets disperse into the vivarium. It is important that the insects are eaten when still coated with the supplement.

For rapid growth and good weight maintenance, many leopard gecko owners and breeders keep a mealworm-filled dish with powdered supplement in the enclosure at all times. Again, this diet can be supplemented once or twice a week by offering crickets or other food items, such as pink mice, wax worms, and small amounts of king mealworms for adults only.

Some individuals choose to raise leopard geckos primarily on crickets, which should not be offered ad libitum. If you choose to feed crickets, use only appropriately sized crickets (three-week old crickets for lizards up to four to six months old, then switch to four-week-old insects; adults ten months or older can be fed four- to six-week-old crickets) coated with a supplement. Offer the crickets to juveniles and subadults every one to two days and two to three times a week for adult leopard geckos. If the appropriately sized cricket is selected, no more than three to five crickets per animal should be consumed within fifteen minutes of introduction.

Water

Offer clean water to your leopard geckos two to three times a week using a shallow container, such as a glass ashtray or small, plastic reptile dish. Use smaller containers, such as jar lids or petri dishes, to provide water to juveniles. Leopard geckos should be able to drink water out of a dish in the same manner as a dog or cat, but they cannot readily drink from tall containers where the water is out of sight. It is a good idea to remove the water container after a few hours.

If water is allowed to remain in the vivarium at all times, change it two to three times a week to prevent bacterial growth and fecal contamination. At least once a week, or whenever the water has been fouled, wash the water container with an antibacterial dish detergent. Rinse thoroughly before adding new water. Once a month, disinfect water dishes by soaking them for thirty to sixty minutes in a 5-percent bleach solution. Again, rinse thoroughly before use.

Munching Mealworms

Mealworms make a fairly good diet for leopard geckos. Animals exclusively fed mealworms for the first few years of their lives obtained most of the leopard gecko longevity records. Apparently, leopard geckos can achieve substantial life spans with diets consisting primarily of these insects. No study to date has proven that crickets or other insects are more beneficial to leopard geckos.

CHAPTER 7

SHEDDING AND TAIL LOSS

This high yellow leopard gecko has a regenerated tail.

Like other reptiles, leopard geckos periodically shed their entire epithelial skin (outer layer of the skin). Between shed cycles, when leopard geckos replace the superficial layers of their skin, the skin of leopard geckos is in a resting stage that ends when the cells that generate the new skin begin to divide. This starts the actual shed cycle and, as can be expected, the process affects the coloration of leopard geckos. As the shed cycle begins, the skin becomes duller. The skin becomes progressively dull until the underlying new skin is fully formed and the superficial old skin begins to separate from it. At this point, the gecko looks like it is covered with a thin, papery membrane. The old skin then starts detaching itself in sheetlike sections, much like skin peeling after a sunburn. Like many geckos, leopard geckos seize the peeling sections in their mouths and consume them, possibly to ingest certain nutrients contained in the skin. In the wild, eating the skin probably reduces scent markers that attract potential predators such as snakes and predatory mammals. The coloration of leopard geckos is brightest right after they have shed.

Shedding Problems

Geckos that fail to shed look dull and pale and show obvious signs of adhering old skin on the body, eyelids, and extremities. They also tend to be listless. Failure to shed indicates a serious problem in geckos and can result in death if not quickly addressed. Low temperatures, a lack or abundance of vitamin A, weakness caused by injury, bacterial infections, parasites, metabolic bone disease, and low relative humidity are all factors that contribute to shedding problems. Provide proper diet supplementation to eliminate any dietary causes and provide a humidified shelter to ensure that adequate humidity is available for your leopard gecko to shed properly. Close observation of your leopard gecko, including its feces, level of activity, and weight loss or gain, will allow you to determine whether it has a bacterial or parasitic disease. A qualified veterinarian should be consulted for proper diagnosis and treatment.

If ignored, failure to shed can result in eye problems, the loss or infections of digits, and, in extreme cases, death. You can use a cotton swab dipped in hydrogen peroxide to soften and gently remove the adherent skin but caution must be taken to prevent getting peroxide into the eyes. For skin that is still firmly attached, moisturize it with an ophthalmic (eye) lubricant ointment. Once softened, the pieces can be gently removed but should never be forced. The digits appear to be the most susceptible to vascular damage and retained sheds will lead to their sloughing. Shedding problems are best prevented by the use of a moist hide box. A mini humidity chamber can be constructed from a Tupperware container with an entry and exit hole cut into it. Fill the inside of the chamber with vermiculite or sphagnum moss. Humidity chambers also serve as a site for females to lay their eggs.

Tail Loss (Caudal Autotomy)

Like most geckos, leopard geckos will drop their tails if threatened or grabbed by the tail. Following autotomy, the original tail will twitch on the ground. In the wild, the squirming tail holds the attention of a predator and provides a snack while the leopard gecko escapes. The caudal (tail) vertebrae of leopard geckos have connective tissue fracture points that allow the tail or a section of the tail to autotomize easily. This process is accompanied by rapid vasoconstriction, which minimizes blood loss. Although leopard geckos can grow new tails, what replaces the original tail section is a bulbous unringed structure, no longer supported by bony vertebrae but instead by a cartilaginous rod. The regrown tail is not as aesthetically pleasing as the original. It tends to be shorter and acquires proportions that make it resemble the head. If attacked again, a leopard gecko can drop the entire regrown section.

Tail loss is not only caused by predator attacks but also by intraspecies aggression (being attacked by a member of its own species): male leopard geckos may attack each other; babies may drop their tails during a feeding frenzy or fight; and aggressive females may cause tail loss as may overzealous sexually aggressive males. When a leopard gecko drops its tail, it loses a significant amount of fat reserve and is more vulnerable to stress. The leopard gecko should be removed and kept by itself in a separate enclosure until its tail has regenerated. The tailless animal must be kept warm, fed, and watered regularly. Examine the conditions that caused the tail loss and make the necessary steps to prevent it from reoccurring.

CHAPTER 8

THE RECOGNITION AND TREATMENT OF DISEASE

Roger Klingenberg, D.V.M.

L eopard geckos are very hardy lizards, making their visits to the reptile veterinarian few and far between. With proper husbandry, most medical problems can be avoided. However, some problems may be encountered and these merit discussion.

A healthy leopard gecko has clear eyes and no nasal secretions.

Hypocalcemia (Metabolic Bone Disease)

Leopard geckos are somewhat more resistant to complications from low calcium levels (hypocalcemia) than most other commonly kept lizards. The signs include lethargy, weakness, painful movement, a softened or "rubbery" jaw, and swollen or distorted limbs. The lack of a calcium

35

supplement with appropriate levels of vitamin D_3 is the most common cause. Being primarily insectivores, it is imperative that leopard geckos be provided insects that have been dusted with the appropriate supplements. While calcium supplements need to have a greater calcium content than phosphorus, reptile veterinarians are seeing the benefits of using calcium products that do not contain any phosphorus. Daily calcium carbonate dustings for juveniles and every other day dustings for adults work well. Once a week, a calcium/D_3 supplement should replace the calcium carbonate dusting. If signs of hypocalcemia are noted, then vitamin D_3 dustings can be increased until you see an improvement. However, vitamin D_3 in excessive levels can cause soft tissue mineralization, so use good judgment and do not oversupplement. Feeding pink mice once every two weeks also provides an excellent source of vitamins and minerals, including calcium and preformed vitamin D_3. Avoid excessive feeding of pink mice as it can lead to obesity.

Gastroenteritis/Diarrhea
The most obvious sign of gastrointestinal disease is weight loss combined with the presence of undigested cricket masses, instead of the standard, relatively dry feces. The cricket masses may be a result of regurgitation or the passing of undigested prey. Other signs of gastrointestinal disorders include lethargy, anorexia, and unusually watery or bloody stools. Leopard geckos may also demonstrate a darkening of the iris (colored portion of the eye). Severely affected animals that have stopped eating and drinking are at great risk of dying. A veterinarian can help determine the cause of the gastrointestinal crisis. Most gastroenteritis cases are due to bacterial infections; a fecal culture may be required to help select an effective drug. It is important to have a fecal sample examined for intestinal parasites, such as trichomonads and coccidia.

Trichomonads are flagellate protozoans that can be treated with metronidazole (Flagyl or Searle) at a dosage of 50 mg/kg daily for three to five days. Coccidia are another matter and much more difficult to eliminate.

Coccidia

The fact that geckos thrive in small containers makes them particularly susceptible to coccidia. Coccidia are tiny protozoan parasites that invade the intestinal lining in order to reproduce. The product of their reproduction is a tiny egglike structure called an oocyst. The oocyst is the infective stage of the parasite and is passed with the fecal matter into the environment in the hopes that another host will become exposed to it. In a small, closed environment, geckos can repeatedly act as the host, with the numbers of coccidia increasing exponentially. When a parasite with a direct life cycle (no intermediate hosts required) builds up like this, it is referred to as a super-infection. The irritation to the gastrointestinal tract leads to dehydration and anorexia and allows secondary bacteria to invade. Treatment consists of giving a sulfa-based drug. The best is sulfadimethoxine (Albon) at 50 mg/kg orally every twenty-four to forty-eight hours until resolved.

Medication alone, however, is insufficient. Fastidious cleaning is essential for coccidia to be fully resolved. Set up an extra cage and switch the gecko back and forth between cages once or twice a day. Use newspaper as a substrate for easy cleaning and eliminate all elaborate cage furniture while the animal is being treated. Follow-up fecal exams are important to make sure the coccidia are eliminated. This is a very contagious parasite, passing easily from gecko to gecko, so all new additions to a colony should be strictly quarantined while evaluated for parasites.

Digit and Dermal Infections

Chronic shed problems can destroy the vascular pattern in the toes and result in the loss of digits. These traumatized and inflamed toes can become further insulted by exposure to substrate medium that is too moist or dirty. Not only will the toes become infected but also superficial skin infections, seen as discolored areas, may occur. The first step in resolving this problem is to address its cause. Replace soiled substrate media with newspaper or paper toweling until the infection clears. Mild, superficial skin problems can be treated with a neomycin and polymyxin B antibiotic cream, such as Polysporin or Neosporin, but severe cases will require veterinary intervention. Once healed, place the leopard gecko in a cage with a clean, dry medium.

Stomatitis or Mouthrot

Stomatitis is often a primary mouth disease in reptiles. However, in leopard geckos stomatitis is usually exhibited secondary to fighting. Symptoms include swelling, malocclusion (uneven upper and lower jaw), and a failure to eat well. On close inspection, caseated (cheeselike) pus can be seen.

Clean the mouth with hydrogen peroxide or a dilute liquid antiseptic (Betadine), gently removing all loose tissue and pus. An extremely light layer of neomycin and polymyxin B antibiotic cream can be applied daily, but it can be toxic in excessive quantities. In all but the mildest cases, consult a veterinarian. Systemic antibiotics are generally required to resolve difficult cases.

Respiratory Infections

As is true with all reptiles, excessively cool temperatures (under 74° F) for excessive periods of time will cause immune system suppression with subsequent respiratory infections. Symptoms may be subtle and include a partial opening of the mouth with labored expiration. Initially, a temperature change to a daytime high of 84–86° F with a drop at night to no lower than 80° F may be adequate for mild cases. If improvement is not seen or symptoms worsen, consult a veterinarian.

Egg Binding

Occasionally a leopard gecko will fail to pass one of the two eggs typically formed. While you may be tempted to manipulate the egg out, this is difficult to do without the reproductive tract being irreversibly torn. Reproductive hormones, such as oxytocin, don't seem to resolve the problem.

It is best to have the remaining egg removed surgically. Egg binding may be due in part to hypocalcemia; calcium is essential to the contraction of the reproductive smooth muscle. Gravid females should be fed calcium supplements daily.

CHAPTER 9

BREEDING

Leopard geckos are the easiest to breed of all the lizards currently offered in the herpetoculture trade. In fact, they will often breed even if you make no special efforts for them to do so.

When to Breed

As with many reptiles, size is more important than age as the primary criterion for a leopard gecko reaching sexual maturity. Leopard geckos generally reach sexual maturity at a weight of around 35 grams. Many breeders grow their animals to about 40 grams before they breed them. Depending on the temperature at which they are raised, leopard geckos reach maturity between ten and twenty-four months. Most animals in captivity will breed for the first time between fourteen and eighteen months of age.

A leopard gecko hatches.

The albino trait, as shown here, was first recorded in 1996.

Requirements for Successful Breeding

The first condition for successful breeding is to have at least one male leopard gecko and one or more females. The second condition is to have healthy leopard geckos. Leopard geckos that are ill or thin should not be considered for breeding and should be housed individually. Also, they should be fed or treated until they are back to health and have good weight, with tails showing moderate to high fat reserves. Finally, leopard geckos should not be too old. The best breeders are two to three years old. Animals older than six years can breed but produce fewer eggs. Females older than nine years will produce few, if any, eggs.

Prebreeding Conditioning

Prior to breeding, all animals should be in prime condition with a healthy body weight. Many owners do not precondition their animals in any special manner prior to breeding. Others expose their animals to a prebreeding conditioning period consisting of a shorter photoperiod (less than twelve hours of daylight per twenty-four hours) and cooler temperatures (as low as 65° F at night and 72–76° F during the day) for four to eight weeks prior to breeding attempts. Because both cooler temperature and reduced daylight are natural features of winters in most countries, implementing this kind of conditioning requires little effort. Both methods work; however, if you have poor results with one then try implementing the other.

Breeding Season

In captivity, leopard geckos usually breed during a season that extends from January to September. Depending on many factors, some start breeding as early as January while others do not begin breeding until late spring. Some captive leopard geckos begin breeding late in the season, and breed up to and including the month of October. Under controlled conditions, leopard geckos can be made to breed at any time of the year with the exception of a three- to four-month rest period.

Group Breeding

Most owners use a group breeding method, housing one male with between ten and twenty females. Some keep one male with as many as fifty females. From a production point of view, this method has a clear economic advantage because you are not wasting resources feeding, raising, and housing large numbers of males. Under these conditions males can be kept with females year round, although some breeders claim better success when they remove males during the few months that leopard geckos are not breeding (October, November, and December).

Carefully monitor all your animals; some females may not compete as well as others for food and may show signs of gradual weight loss. Evidence of fighting and the occasional loss of a tail may require that one or more animals be temporarily removed from a particular group. For those interested in commercial-scale leopard gecko breeding, the group breeding method is the most effective. To maximize production, keep careful records on the production levels of established groups. Poor reproductive performance requires careful evaluation of breeding stock, health status, and husbandry methods. To increase the probability of reproductive success, it is a good idea to alternate males in breeding groups at least once. Not all males are good breeders.

Quarantine all new stock individually in a separate area from established stock. Always wash your hands after handling or maintaining new stock. I have seen several breeders and hobbyists devastated when coccidiosis infected their entire colony. Cryptosporidium (an infection with no known treatment), normally associated with snakes, was diagnosed in a colony of leopard geckos. Heed this warning!

Single Animal Introduction

Breeders interested in carefully controlled pairings to develop new morphs may keep their leopard geckos singly and introduce females to stud males during the breeding season. Females with developing eggs visible through the abdominal wall tend to be more receptive to male breeding attempts. This method allows for controlled breeding that you can track and also tends to be quite effective. Males kept singly will often readily breed when a female is suddenly introduced to its territory. As a rule, only one or two successful copulations in a given season are necessary for a female to produce fertile eggs. Female leopard geckos apparently have the ability to retain sperm for up to a year. Another advantage to this method is that when females are maintained singly, except for short reproductive encounters, they experience less stress because males do not continually pester them.

Breeding Diet

Breeding imposes considerable energy demands and calcium demands on females. During breeding, offer females food coated with a vitamin/mineral mix at least every other day or have mealworms in a vitamin/mineral powder offered in dishes around the clock. Dishes of powdered calcium carbonate, calcium gluconate, or a calcium/D_3 mix should always be available. To help females regain weight during the breeding season, provide one- to two-day-old pink mice, the rumps dipped in calcium.

Herp trends are fast moving. What is rare and valuable today may be old hat tomorrow.

Egg-Laying and Incubation

Egg Clutches

Leopard geckos typically produce multiple clutches of two eggs during the breeding season. Occasionally, single egg clutches are laid, usually from very young or older females. As a rule, young geckos produce one to three clutches during their first year; as they mature, they will produce up to five clutches of eggs. Breeders who have made concerted efforts to maintain their animals under optimal conditions have reported animals laying up to eight clutches of fertile eggs a year. After several years of peak breeding, older leopard geckos tend to gradually produce fewer eggs and fertility is decreased. Eventually, old leopard geckos stop breeding altogether.

The V-shaped row of enlarged pre-anal pores on the gecko at the top indicates it's a male; the bottom gecko is a female

Egg-Laying

As female leopard geckos get closer to depositing eggs, the developing eggs within the female become more clearly defined and cause slight bulging at the sides of the abdomen. Breeders use two methods for collecting eggs. One is to simply leave the setup as is: mist the inside of the shelter daily so that the ground medium is slightly damp, and check the setup once or twice a day for eggs that may have been deposited within or outside the shelter.

Other breeders prefer to construct an egg-laying chamber consisting of a plastic container half-filled with vermiculite or sand. Water is added so that it is moist but not soggy. The covered container must be large enough for the female to enter. A hole is cut in the side of the container just above the layer of moistened medium. Often, but not always, a female will select this egg-laying chamber as a laying site. The advantage of this method is that if a female utilizes the chamber, the eggs are not likely to desiccate (dry out). This can also help save time by not having to look throughout the entire enclosure for the eggs.

Freshly laid leopard gecko eggs tend to be somewhat soft and sticky. Fertile eggs quickly firm up and are covered with a thick, leathery, chalk-white membrane while infertile eggs often remain thin and soft and fail to become turgid.

Incubation of Eggs

For proper egg incubation, the leopard gecko eggs must absorb moisture primarily from the high relative humidity of the atmosphere. High relative humidity will cause them to gain weight, but an incubating medium that is too moist can result in too much internal water pressure within the egg and possibly be attacked by molds. When this happens, the shell appears stretched and semitransparent.

One common way to incubate eggs is to use a plastic shoebox or sweater-sized plastic storage box with 1-to 1½-inches of barely moistened, coarse vermiculite or a vermiculite/perlite mix (50:50) added as an incubating medium. The proper moisture level is obtained by mixing six parts mix with four parts water (6:4), by weight. Many breeders simply add water to the medium and mix it by hand until it feels damp but not wet. Place the eggs on their sides and half bury them within the medium. A small container of water, such as a jar lid, can be placed on top of the medium to maintain a high relative air humidity. Place a lid on the storage box. Most lids are loose enough that there will still be some air flow, but if you do not plan on regularly opening the box to check the eggs, drill tiny holes in the upper portion of each side for ventilation.

Incubators

Other methods for incubation include the use of a small poultry incubator, such as a Hova Bator, or making a homemade incubator with a submersible aquarium heater.

To construct a homemade incubator, simply purchase a submersible aquarium heater (75–100 watt is suitable for smaller incubators). Place it at the bottom of an aquarium (at least a standard 20-gallon vivarium is recommended) and add water to a height of ½ inch to 2 inches above the heater. Build a platform above the water level to set your egg-incubating containers on. There are various methods of doing this: some people simply use a couple of bricks on which a section of thick, welded-wire fencing is placed, while others construct a Plexiglas structure that can easily be taken in and out of the aquarium. The incubating container, with

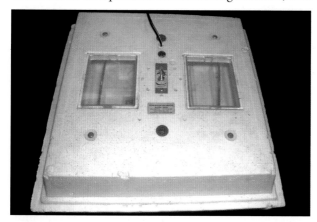

The Hova-Bator is an inexpensive incubator popular with gecko breeders.

The Hova-Bator includes a thermostat and thermometer for adjusting the temperature. With viewing windows you can monitor the inside temperature and state of the incubating eggs.

eggs, will eventually be placed on the platform. Finally, a tight-fitting cover of polystyrene foam should be constructed to cover the top of the aquarium incubator.

The principle for this type of incubator is simple: a submersible heater within a low level of water in the aquarium heats up the air above the water to the desired temperature. You just have to develop a method of suspending the egg containers inside the heated air. The key, of course, is proper calibration of the submersible heater. To do this, you must first calibrate the incubator with an empty container (you don't want to overheat your eggs).

If you use a poultry incubator, place moistened vermiculite and a small water container at the bottom.

Calibrating Incubators

Whether you are using a poultry incubator or a homemade incubator, you must calibrate the thermostat to the desired temperature. The key is using a good thermometer inside the container. Electronic digital thermometers with thermal sensors (for outside temperature) are available in electronic supply stores and through mail order reptile supply companies. The cost of these thermometers ranges between $15 and $30, depending on their features. The most expensive will give a daily minimum and maximum temperature reading. Some even have an alarm system that beeps to warn you when the temperature goes above or below a given setting. Keep the digital thermometer outside of the incubator where it can be easily read, then place the sensor inside the incubating container and switch to the "out" reading. This will allow for a continuous readout of the temperature. By contrast, a standard thermometer will require you to open the container to get an accurate reading. As a backup, use an inexpensive standard thermometer to occasionally verify the readings. Whatever thermometer you are using, calibration will require small adjustments to the thermostatic control of the incubator.

Once set, let the incubator run awhile before proceeding with the next adjustment. To be safe, allow up to an hour for the temperature to settle to the new thermostat adjustment. Calibrating an incubator can take quite a bit of time, so do this before the eggs are laid. Proper calibrating of the incubator is critical to your hatching success. Recently, on-off thermostats (e.g., from Zoo Med) have become available in the general trade. With these thermostats, if the recorded temperature goes above or below the set temperature, the heating unit is turned off. These are the least expensive and most widely used thermostats. The more advanced pulse-proportional thermostats are available mostly by mail order through Helix Control, Bush Herpetological Supply, and other herpetological supply companies. They allow you to easily and very precisely set and maintain desired incubator temperatures. The temperature readings are taken steadily and the heating device is controlled by an electronic rheostat, which regulates the current of the unit to produce the desired level of heat.

Incubation Temperatures

Recent studies by Brian Viets, Ph.D., and others have confirmed that leopard gecko sex is determined by temperature within the first two weeks of incubation. If the eggs are incubated at a temperature of 79° F, most of the offspring will be female. At temperatures of 85–87° F, there will be a more or less equal ratio of males and females. At 90° F, the great majority of the hatchlings will be males. Herpetoculturists, depending on their goals, should determine the preferred incubation temperature(s) for their specific purposes. To obtain males, incubate eggs at 89–90° F for the first three to four weeks and then incubate them at cooler temperatures—80–85° F—to reduce any risk of mortality from incubating the eggs too close to their warmer temperature limits (95° F). When large-scale breeding for the pet trade is the primary goal, breeding for females is more desirable because they can be kept together in groups. *See Chapter 10.*

Incubating eggs should be checked on a regular basis, as should the incubating medium and any water containers. Depending on incubation temperatures, leopard gecko eggs will hatch in six to fifteen weeks.

Raising Juveniles

Ideally, juvenile leopard geckos should be housed individually in plastic shoeboxes with a small shelter and a shallow water dish. If housed in groups, hatchling leopard geckos must be segregated by size to prevent feeding competition. As a rule, larger or more dominant leopard geckos chase prey more vigorously and intimidate smaller leopard geckos. The result in a mixed colony of babies is that some animals grow much faster and therefore compete more effectively for available food items (bigger also means needing to eat more). Small animals may remain small and eventually start to decline. Keeping babies in large containers, offering plenty of food, and segregating by size will help prevent these kinds of problems.

During the first week following hatching, baby leopard geckos live off of their yolk reserves. They do not begin feeding until after their first shed, which should occur within the first week of hatching. Hatchlings and juveniles should be fed three-week-old vitamin/mineral supplemented crickets every one to two days. Half-grown mealworms with calcium powder can also be offered in feeding dishes that prevent the mealworm from escaping. A shallow water dish should be available at all times. In addition, lightly misting the inside of shelters two to three times a week is recommended to increase relative air humidity and to facilitate shedding.

How Important Is Heat?

In one study, leopard gecko hatchlings that were provided with a heat source for thermoregulation grew one and a half times as fast as a group maintained at a constant 78° F. (Autum and De Nardo, 1995)

CHAPTER 10

INCUBATION TEMPERATURE AND HATCHLING SEX AND PIGMENTATION

Brian E. Viets, Ph.D.

Temperature-Dependent Sex Determination

In most vertebrates, sex is determined at fertilization, usually by chromosomes. This mode of sex determination is termed genotypic sex determination (GSD). However, in the leopard gecko and the African fat-tailed gecko, the incubation temperature of the egg determines the sex of the hatchling. This type of sex determination is termed temperature-dependent sex determination (TSD) and is a well-documented phenomenon occurring in all crocodilians, most turtles, and some lizards.

Although the leopard gecko and the African fat-tailed gecko are closely related, not all closely related geckos have the same mode of sex determination. In fact, two other closely related eublepharid geckos, the Texas banded gecko *(Coleonyx brevis)* and the banded gecko, have GSD.

Both the leopard gecko and the African fat-tailed gecko have a Pattern II type of TSD; females are produced predominantly at cool temperatures, males are produced pre-

dominantly at intermediate temperatures, and females are again produced predominantly at warm temperatures (see Fig. 1). Pattern II TSD is sometimes referred to as Pattern FMF (females at cool temperatures, males at intermediate temperatures, and females at warm temperatures). For both species, some females can be produced at all temperatures; there is no set temperature that produces 100 percent males. This appears to be the norm in TSD species.

The studies that my colleagues and I perform use constant incubation temperatures, with temperatures in the incubators varying no more than 32.36° F from the desired temperature. As these types of incubators are rarely available to hobbyists, it is important to realize the effect of varying incubation temperatures. Fluctuating incubation temperatures can substantially affect sex ratios—the greater the degree of variation, the greater the potential impact on sex ratio. In fact, the same mean incubation temperature can produce 100 percent males or 100 percent females, depending on the degree of variation from the mean.

In a species with Pattern II TSD, there are two temperatures that produce equal numbers of females and males. These two temperatures are termed pivotal temperatures. However, individual mothers may have very different pivotal temperatures. For instance, in leopard geckos, 87° F typically produces an equal number of females and males. However, in some mothers, 100 percent female offspring are produced at 87° F, and for others, 100 percent males are produced. (Geckos have a fixed clutch size of two eggs, so all offspring produced by a given mother in a year must be recorded. Each individual clutch can only produce two females, two males, or one of each.) The numbers shown in Fig. 1 are the result of over five thousand egg incubations, so the sex-determining curves represent population responses. The particular pattern of individual mothers may vary.

Duration of Incubation and Viable Incubation Temperatures

Incubation temperature significantly influences the duration of incubation in all lizards. In both leopard geckos and African fat-tailed geckos, incubation temperature and mean days to hatching are inversely correlated, meaning that at higher temperatures the incubation period is shorter. In leopard geckos, the incubation period ranges from 36 days at 90.5° F to 107 days at 75° F (longer incubation periods would be expected when incubation temperature varies). At 93–95° F developmental rate slows, so the incubation period is actually longer. The lethal minimum constant incubation temperature for leopard geckos lies just below 75° F, and the lethal maximum constant incubation temperature lies just above 95° F.

Fig. 1

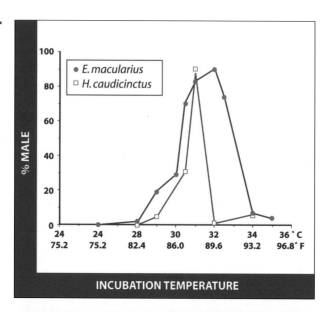

INCUBATION TEMPERATURE

Studies show that incubation temperature may have an effect on black dorsal pigmentation.

High Incubation Temperatures and Female Behavior

In 1988, Gutzke and Crews reported that incubation temperature affects not only the sex, but also the endocrine physiology and reproductive behavior of adult female leopard geckos. Adult females incubated at 78.8° F (an exclusively female-producing temperature) and 84.2° F (a

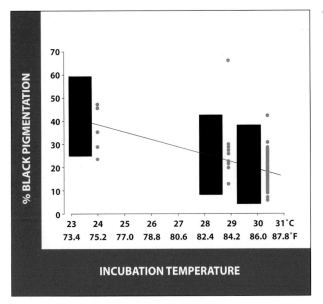

Fig. 2

mostly female-producing temperature) differed both hormonally and behaviorally from females incubated at 89.6° F (a mostly male-producing temperature). These "hot females" were more likely to exhibit aggressive behavior and none of them laid eggs during the study.

Two subsequent studies (Viets et al., 1993, and Tousignant et al., 1995) failed to support these findings. No hormonal differences were observed between females from different incubation temperatures, and all high temperature females in these studies produced viable offspring. However, incubation temperature has a profound effect on the onset of reproduction. Females from lower incubation temperatures reach sexual maturation at an earlier age than do females from higher incubation temperatures. The females in Gutzke and Crews' study were not sexually mature and therefore prematurely diagnosed as being functionally sterile.

The Effects of Incubation Temperature and Heritability on Pigmentation
In temperature-dependent sex determination studies in the leopard gecko, the black dorsal pigmentation varied

Several factors, including genetics, incubation temperature, and stress, affect the pigmentation of a leopard gecko.

greatly between siblings that had been incubated at 82.4° F and 93° F (see Fig. 2). Similar variations have been reported in turtles and alligators. Thus, incubation temperature seemed to be a determining factor in the amount of black pigmentation. However, incubation temperature was not the only factor. Siblings hatched from the same temperature often had noticeable differences in the amount of black pigmentation.

In order to assess the degree to which incubation temperature affected pigmentation in leopard geckos, lizards were videotaped in a standard position, then the images were digitized. The percentage of black pigmentation was calculated by dividing the number of black pixels by the total pixels in the image. A regression plot of the percentage of black pigmentation in hatchlings versus incubation temperature yielded a highly significant negative slope, meaning that lower incubation temperatures produced significantly darker hatchlings than did higher incubation temperatures (see Fig. 2).

However, because leopard geckos have temperature-dependent sex determination, sex and incubation temperature are confounded variables. To investigate whether sex affected pigmentation independently of incubation temperature, animals produced at 87° F—a temperature that produces both sexes—were examined. No significant differences were found between males and females with regards to the percentage of black pigmentation.

We also examined heritability of pigmentation patterns. First, the amount of black pigmentation in both parents was determined and then these values were compared with the amount of black pigmentation in their offspring. Narrow-sense heritability of black pigmentation was 27.1 percent, meaning that 27.1 percent of the pigmentation pattern of individual geckos was genetic. Darker parents tend to have darker offspring.

So, the pigmentation pattern of a gecko is due in large part to two things: the pigmentation patterns of the parents (which was expected) and environmental effects, such as incubation temperature (which wasn't necessarily expected). Interestingly, there are other environmental factors that have an effect on pigmentation. The young, high-yellow leopard gecko that you have today may turn into a mediocre-looking gecko as the breeding season wears on. Stress hormones (e.g. corticosterone) affect pigmentation, causing an animal to lose its bright coloration and become somewhat drab. Few breeding adults maintain the intensity of color that they exhibit as yearlings. In addition, recent studies by herpetologist Larry Talent have demonstrated that crowding (again, a stress-inducer) affects pigmentation in juveniles. Hatchlings grown in crowded conditions tend to be much less colorful than those raised in isolation.

Although there are obviously some genetic components to pigmentation patterns in leopard geckos, the incubation environment, post-hatching environment, and stress of breeding can have a significant effect as well. Unless you know the incubation history and lineage of a particular gecko, leopard gecko morphs should be viewed with some caution.

CHAPTER 11

COLOR AND PATTERN VARIATIONS

Ron Tremper

I t is safe to say that the leopard gecko is the most widely bred terrarium reptile in the world. So, it is no surprise that its genetic possibilities would emerge and develop through the growing field of herpetoculture.

As of 1990, the only variation available in the pet trade was the high-yellow morph. This morph was merely a normal patterned gecko with an intense yellow or gold color predominating the body, sometimes with small amounts of orange around the top of the tail base.

In 1978, I acquired my first adult geckos. As of this writing, these geckos have been bred to the twentieth generation without any additional stocks being added. These geckos were line bred, which is to say that they were of one large, related family group or lineage. Such breeding practices eventually express any recessive or hidden traits in a given population. But it was not until 1991 that a baby randomly hatched with two black, longitudinal body stripes, running from the head to the base of the tail. This partial striped female was then bred back to its father and the result was the first striped and first jungle-phase geckos. These offspring were the first geckos I had ever seen with a tail pattern other than the normal four or five rings. They had dorsally isolated tail blotches of white and one had a complete straight-edged white stripe to the tip of the tail.

Many variations quickly emerged through selective breeding and the term "designer leopard gecko" was born.

Pattern

From the beginning I chose to select three recessive traits, two of which involved pattern, in my founding stocks of designer geckos. These were reduced numbers of dark head spots, bright body colors of yellow or orange, and aberrant patterns. Basically, I found that the variations discovered in all geckos were the result of simple recessive gene pairings. As a hobbyist, you will get offspring that

This interesting creature is a lavender and yellow leopard gecko.

Another lavender and yellow leopard gecko is shown.

resemble the parents if both parents are mutations themselves. However, if you breed a wild-caught leopard gecko to any known mutation, you will mask the mutation if the wild-type parent is carrying no recessive traits.

There are several morph patterns that are now seen in the leopard gecko pet trade.

Normal: A normal pattern gecko (typical wild morph representative of those found in the wild) has two dark transverse body bands and three to four dark tail rings with numerous dark body and head spots mixed with a light cream or tan color.

The wild-type pattern is fully evident at hatching and becomes obscured with age. The dark bands and rings may appear as shades of purple or violet at sexual maturity. The light cream or tan color is not well defined in any set pattern.

Jungle: The jungle-phase gecko is a highly variable aberrant gecko with irregular, asymmetrical, and dark body blotches and a non-ringed tail. The jungle phase has dark bold spots on the limbs—from this pattern mutation came the first fully striped geckos. The jungle-phase trait is dominant over the striped trait.

A jungle-phase female produced in 1994 was hatched with a uniquely shaped head and a blunt tail about two-thirds the length of a normal tail. The animal was sterile. This condition is probably genetically linked to her peculiar body shape.

The jungle leopard gecko is a morph characterized by an irregular dorsal pattern and an unringed tail.

Striped: The striped gecko is an aberrant gecko with a light-colored longitudinal dorsal stripe. The stripe joins with the white neck ring and runs to the base of the tail or tail tip.

This morph speaks for itself and is a very common mutation in many species of reptiles, particularly snakes. In a true "striper" the vertebral light-colored stripe joins completely with the white neck ring; otherwise it is consid-

The striped leopard gecko was derived through selective breeding from jungle phase leopards. As a rule, it is difficult to genetically fix pattern morphs.

ered a partial stripe morph. The stripe phase never has a normally ringed tail pattern. The tail may either be entirely or partially striped or blotched.

Reverse Stripe: This is an aberrant gecko with a dark colored longitudinal dorsal stripe, which joins with the white neck ring and may be broken at the tail base. The tail is predominately white with dark dorsal blotches or striping.

As the name implies, this pattern morph displays a

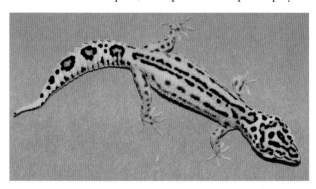

A reverse-striped leopard gecko shows its stripes.

complete reversal of the body and tail colors. This morph was first developed in 1997.

Patternless: This aberrant gecko lacks all dark pigment markings and patterns and has normal colored eyes.

In 1991, a California breeder announced a strange gecko he had produced from seemingly normal appearing parents. This gave rise to the so-called leucistic morph that

has become so popular. This gecko hatches out with large brown or tan blotches over a very pale or cream-colored body. With growth, as in all leopard geckos, the blotches are lost through the movement of pigment cells in the skin. The result is a striking gecko with a light yellow body and head and tail coloring that is lighter than the cream color it hatched with.

All leopard geckos can change color to some extent, but when you remove the darker pigments these color changes are much more evident. A top-quality leucistic can look like a bronze colored lizard one moment and an exquisite light-colored gem the next. Some examples of this form, however, stay dark brown as adults. Other variations of patternless are geckos missing all dark body spots and bands but are from a different gene than the leucistic.

Notice the lack of dark pattern on this adult patternless leopard gecko.

The yellow-orange leopard gecko is another beautiful morph.

Color

Color variation is one of the most important aspects of the current rage in designer and mutation leopard geckos. The bright blue or turquoise color seen on the top of the head and between the eyes of hatchling geckos is normal and fades, then disappears, with age.

Normal: This gecko has black, brown, shades of purple, and cream coloration. The wild-caught or normal-phase geckos are a mixture of subdued black, brown, and shades of purple, with a light cream or tan coloration lacking intensity. Wild populations contain numerous recessive genes that herpetoculturists are expressing as new phenotypes (the observable physical characteristics) each year.

Shown is another example of the outstanding yellow-orange line developed by Bill Brant.

The high-yellow leopard gecko is a very popular morph.

High Yellow: This type of gecko has an extremely bright yellow or gold background coloration, with any pattern phase.

Coined names such as "golden" and "hyperxanthic" are one and the same morph but may represent different lines of breeding. The high-yellow morph is extremely beautiful when the color is seen on animals that lack most of the small dark body and head spots. The color can appear on all of the known pattern variations.

High yellows can be determined at hatching by examining the hind legs. If the femur (the area from the body to the knee joint) is entirely yellow—missing the traditional dark streak on top of the leg—in color, then the newborn will become a high yellow. This recognition tool is very useful for selecting favored animals.

Orange/Tangerine: This gecko has an orange pigment anterior to the tail base.

These are representatives of lines developed by David Nieves. On top is a tangerine leopard gecko and on the bottom is a high-contrast leopard gecko with orange tint.

Orange and tangerine represent the same variation but are a lineage developed by different breeders through selective efforts. Actually, they are offshoots of the same gene.

Several private colonies were line bred for numerous years to obtain this orange coloration anterior to the tail-base. Orange color, to varying degrees, was common on leopard gecko tails but it was not until 1996 that breeders succeeded in getting any significant amounts of orange on the body in adults. Future efforts will probably result in animals that are totally orange and black, orange and purple, and orange and yellow. Even a totally bright red gecko is possible.

White: In adults, black and white colors predominate. The hypomelanistic (lacking melanin) or "snow" geckos fall into this class of gecko color variation. Such animals are black and white at hatching and remain that way as adults. The amount of black pigment can vary due to selective breeding, and white geckos may be represented by any pattern morph.

White leopard geckos are also marketed as "snow" leopard geckos.

Lavender: This coloration is indicated when adults have shades of purple predominately on the body and tail, with a cream or yellow background.

The "lavenders" are a natural result of the changes that occur in all dark—almost black—birth bands on the body and tail regions. Pigment cells migrate as the gecko

grows and the result can be vivid, large, purplish blotches on a light-cream or high-yellow background. At hatching, lavender hatchlings resemble normal or banded high-yellow phase.

Ghost: A ghost gecko is of any pattern phase with extremely faded colors and greatly reduced dark pigmentation.

Animals with this color only express it after they reach the size of 5 to 6 inches total length. They start out looking like dark-colored hatchlings, but with each passing month,

their color lightens and fades. This is a very pale, healthy gecko morph with genetically caused fading, not to be confused with a female at the end of the egg-laying season whose natural colors fade due to nutritional depletion.

Melanistic: The melanistic gecko is predominately black with any pattern phase.

Several breeders are developing black phase geckos. The young have white lips and all-black hind limbs at birth, and the spaces between the dominant body markings turn a dark yellow as they mature.

Amelanistic: This is an albino gecko that genetically lacks melanin. It can be of any pattern phase. For decades, herpetoculturists dreamed of the world's first commercially available albino leopard gecko. In September of 1996, the first albino to hatch in captivity occurred randomly through the incidental crossing of two heterozygous (normal looking) wild-imported geckos by a California breeder. This animal was a female banded morph and shared an isolated egg cup with her heterozygous brother. Captive breed-

A baby albino leopard gecko poses for the camera.

ing efforts of this unique and rare mutation continued and albinos are now readily available in the hobbyist trade.

Additionally, and quite amazingly, a male albino occurred randomly in 1998 from a Nevada breeder. The male's parents can be traced back to that very same group of 1996 wild-imported adults.

It is safe to say that other geckos heterozygous for albinism are living in some of the very homes of people reading this chapter. We do know that at least four "heteros" were in that now-famous shipment. So, who knows, you may be the next surprised gecko keeper.

Leucistic: The leucistic is a white gecko of any pattern phase that has black or blue eyes. A true leucistic gecko is one that has totally white pigment over all of its skin as an adult. It differs from the patternless animals in that surface of the skin is dominated by iridophores (iridophores contribute color through their physical properties causing the diffraction of light to reflect).

Conclusion

The art of herpetoculture has a tremendous palette for anyone to embrace. The selective breeding of leopard geckos is a new frontier awaiting the beginner as well as the advanced breeder. The koi carp of lizards has arrived.

CHAPTER 12

COMMERCIAL BREEDING

All areas of agricultural production require careful research and evaluation. You need to ask yourself what it is you want to do: produce leopard geckos commercially on a large scale or produce the more valuable morphs on a smaller scale. Again, a comparison can be made with goldfish and koi carp production. The focus of the endeavor on the specialist level is aesthetic. It caters to how combinations of color and pattern affect the human mind. As with goldfish, there is a very large commercial market that is an outlet for mass-produced forms.

It is difficult to predict breeding outcome by observing the hatchlings. You might have a high-yellow, jungle, or striped hatchling, but the qualities of the adult cannot be fully predicted. For the morphs to become well established and to maintain the vigor of the species, culling, outbreeding, and introducing new blood is important. While morphs that have large commercial appeal depend on selection by the general buying public, the values of new and expensive morphs are determined by the breeder/specialist market.

Selecting Breeder Stock

As mentioned earlier, hatchling leopard geckos do not fully reflect what the adults will become. The advantage to starting off with hatchlings is that you can purchase them substantially cheaper than subadults, and you will also know the age of your stock. It is a gamble because the animals

may not end up exactly as what you had in mind. On the other hand, they could be even nicer than you expected.

Subadults or young adults are generally more expensive but you will pretty much know what your adults will look like. You also won't have to wait so long before they start producing, potentially returning your initial investment within the first year. Finally, you will still know the age of the animals you are buying. A generally risky proposition is buying large adults or retired breeders. The advantage is that you will know what the animals look like. The disadvantage is they may be old and have low productivity.

The Value of Males

For introducing genetic mutations in captive breeding projects, male leopard geckos are valuable in the same way as an award-winning stallion or bull. Assume, for example, that you have a colony of leopard geckos and that you want to commercially breed the new amelanistic (albino) line. If you buy a single hatchling male and introduce it to fifty normal females, within fourteen months you could produce five hundred animals heterozygous for albinism. Another twenty-four months and the mature heterozygous offspring would be able to produce at least a thousand albinos (four years, or two generations, is about the average length of time that a new leopard gecko mutation can maintain a high value before prices decline). In contrast, if you purchased a single female you would have had between ten and twelve heterozygous hatchlings the first breeding, and twenty-four months later around twenty-five albino hatchlings. The value of males for introducing new genetic material to a colony is evident. On the other hand, few males are needed for large-scale production and breeders often choose to limit the number of males produced by temperature, manipulating the sex determination of captive-bred offspring. In the economic scheme of things, ordinary male leopard geckos are no more valuable, and possibly less valuable, than females. However, outstanding males are worth their weight in gold.

Keeping Records

Successful breeders typically keep records. They record the origins of their adult animals, the date they were obtained, and their age. The number of eggs laid and their laying dates are recorded for individual females or by breeding container. Good breeders also record the parentage of egg clutches and offspring. These records will allow a breeder to determine when annual egg production is declining and whether the breeder stock needs to be replaced for optimal reproduction. It also allows breeders to trace the origins of specific lines, new mutations that may have popped up in their colonies, and to selectively breed lines in a controlled manner. Computers are invaluable for record keeping; there are even software programs specifically designed for herpetoculture records. With computers, breeders can easily input and store information, as well as keep digital photography records.

Managing Breeding Colonies

Leopard gecko colonies take up space and require good management for optimal production. By keeping records, the production of breeding groups is monitored. Successful breeders replace their breeding stock with young captive-raised animals at periodic intervals.

A female has three to four years of peak production, during which time, if kept under optimal conditions, she will produce six to seven clutches of eggs a year—some breeders report up to eight clutches in a peak year. That's a total of fifty-six eggs during peak production. After this, egg clutches start to decline. The following is an example (not representative in its detail, although the overall pattern is accurate) of long-term production for a female leopard gecko. Several factors may account for production levels in a given year but nothing changes the fact that after seven to eight years, production drops significantly.

Year	Eggs
1	0
2	8
3	12
4	16
5	14
6	10
7	10
8	8
9	6
10	4
11	4
12	0
13	0

The maximum number of eggs a female leopard gecko can produce has not yet been determined but is probably between ninety and one hundred. If you want to maximize production in a breeding program, retire females from the colony after seven or eight years. According to Ron Tremper, a good general guideline is to retire and replace females after they have laid seventy eggs.

The Business of Leopard Geckos
Making an income as a commercial herpetoculturist requires marketing and sales. If you want to produce large numbers of inexpensive geckos, then lining up potential buyers such as reptile dealers will be important for the survival of your business. If your focus is to produce relatively

small numbers of valuable morphs, then culling and selective breeding, combined with specialist market targeting, is essential. Exploring various venues for marketing, such as herpetoculture publications, reptile shows, the Internet, international markets, and direct contact, is standard homework for the successful commercial breeder.

My Leopard Geckos Won't Breed!

Surprisingly, questions relating to the failure of leopard geckos to breed are not uncommon. There are many reasons why leopard geckos will not breed, usually associated with husbandry, health, or incompatibility. The following is an overview of reasons why leopard geckos will not breed

- You don't have a sexual pair. Finding out that "Henry" is in fact "Henrietta" is not uncommon among first-time owners of these lizards. So, a first step is to make sure that you have actually put a pair together. Check for preanal pores—if you can't determine the sex, consult your local reptile store or visit your veterinarian.

- The lizards are kept at suboptimal temperatures. Although cooling does not appear to be necessary for leopard geckos to successfully breed, providing adequate heat is.

- They are ill. Various diseases will debilitate leopard geckos, preventing them from accumulating sufficient fat and calcium reserves for egg production. Weak, thin females may have problems laying eggs. High levels of parasites can prevent successful fertilization.

- The geckos are too small and sexually immature, or they are too old and females are post-reproductive.

CHAPTER 13

THE AFRICAN FAT-TAILED GECKO

The African fat-tailed gecko is the second most widely kept and propagated eublepharine gecko. Unlike leopard geckos in the herpetoculture trade, which are primarily captive-bred, the majority of fat-tailed geckos are imported into the United States out of West Africa and require careful acclimation. A significant percentage die as a result of illness and improper care, but once acclimated, and if maintained under proper conditions, African fat-tailed geckos are nearly as hardy as leopard geckos. A velvety appearance combined with rich subtle coloration, large, dark eyes, and a docile personality makes this species one of the best for gecko enthusiasts.

What's in a Name?

The scientific name of the African fat-tailed gecko is *Hemitheconyx caudicinctus* (Etymology: *Hemi* = half or divided; *theconyx* = box claw or nail; *caudicinctus* = ring tailed). Like the leopard gecko, this is another eublepharine possessing moveable eyelids, but this species lacks digital lamellae (transversely expanded scales covered with setae [microscopic hair-like structures with one or more spatulate ends], which form the scansors [toe pads] of geckos, anoles, and one species of skink).

Distribution

Occurs in West Africa; from Nigeria west to Senegal.

Leucistic may be the wrong term to describe the so-called high-yellow leucistic fat-tailed African gecko.

Size

This is another thick-bodied species, like the leopard gecko. Males can grow to 10 inches in total length. Females are seldom longer than 8 inches.

Sexing

Males grow slightly larger than females. A male's head is slightly larger and broader and the neck is somewhat thicker than the female's. The most reliable method of sexing is to turn the animal upside down and look for a V-shaped row of ten to thirteen preanal pores and the presence of hemipenal swellings at the base of the tail in males. Juvenile males can be sexed when they are a few weeks old by checking for the presence of preanal pores with a 10x magnifying glass.

Two pattern morphs are currently recognized in herpetoculture, a banded morph and a white-striped morph characterized by a bright white stripe running down the middle of the back. The white-striped morph is a standard recessive trait. Thus, normal appearing animals can be heterozygous for white stripe and carry the trait. There are now several color morphs of the African fat-tailed gecko. Besides the normal brown, banded morph, there are high-orange African fat-tailed geckos with brown and orange bands, and more recently a morph coined "leucistic," which starts out with pale banded coloration and becomes whitish as it matures.

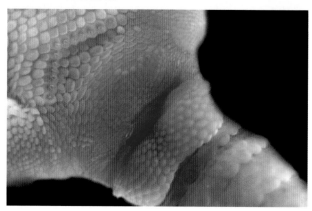

The underside of a male fat-tailed gecko shows preanal pores and hemipenal swellings.

Selection

When selecting African fat-tailed geckos, make sure that they are active, bright-eyed, alert, and have a significant amount of fat reserves in their tails. Avoid imports with thin or broken tails or caked or smeared fecal matter around the vent area. Only experienced herpetoculturists are likely to successfully acclimate animals caught in the wild.

Acclimation

Many imported African fat-tailed geckos are emaciated, dehydrated, stressed, and diseased. Often, imported fat-tailed geckos initially look healthy but start declining in the first weeks following purchase.

The following steps are required for acclimation.

1. House animals individually on paper towels in setups as described below.
2. Keep at 82–85° F.
3. Offer water and food as you would for leopard geckos. Mist lightly every one to two days.
4. If the animal(s) you have selected are losing weight and becoming weak, have their stools checked by a veterinarian as soon as possible. Imported fat-tailed geckos can harbor flagellate protozoans and other causes of gastroenteritis, which must be treated if the animal(s) are to be established. Metronidazole, at a dosage of 100–150 mg/kg orally, can be used successfully in the treatment of flagellate protozoans. Repeat in two weeks.
5. If the lizards are not readily feeding on their own, try the two following procedures. Feed a mixture of banana baby food, Nekton-Tonic (obtainable through specialized reptile stores), and water—mixed to a smooth liquid consistency—with an eyedropper. This mix is usually readily taken by newly imported animals and provides calories, water, and vitamins without the stress of force-feeding. Another liquid diet that is available in drugstores and grocery stores is the protein drink Ensure. To initiate ingestion of these liquid diets, apply a drop on the tip of the snout with an eyedropper. The gecko will lick the drop off and, if the eyedropper tip is

brought close to the mouth, will start licking the liquid as it is slowly pushed out. Do not grab the animal and force its mouth open to pour liquid down its throat; this will do more harm than good.

Another alternative, best used with animals that are relatively vigorous and have a healthy body weight, is to hand-feed them one or two crickets every one to two days. This is an easy process. Prekill a cricket by crushing its head with forceps, then dip it in a vitamin/mineral mix. Take the fat-tailed gecko behind the head with one hand and poke the cricket at the side of the gecko's mouth with the other hand. When you do this, the fat-tailed gecko will probably open its mouth and try to bite sideways. When the gecko's mouth is open, insert the cricket and immediately place the gecko back in its cage. In this manner, most fat tails will eat hand-fed crickets.

With thin animals, water must be available at all times. Instead of offering water, rehydrate by offering one of the many electrolyte solutions now available in the reptile product trade. Try dripping the solution on the snout with an eyedropper to incite lapping.

It is important to stay on top of the situation during the acclimation period, which can last one to two months.

Housing

Housing for fat-tailed geckos is identical to that of leopard geckos, except that it is especially important imported animals be kept singly until well established. As with leopard geckos, females are somewhat compatible in groups but males should never be housed together.

Substrate/Floor Covering
For established African fat-tailed geckos, try using a fine-grade orchid bark or a sandy soil mix as a ground medium. In naturalistic vivaria, they can be kept on a sandy soil mix or a soil/bark/sand mix.

Shelter
The best shelter for fat-tailed geckos is a humidifying shelter. Fill a shallow container (1- to 1½-inches tall), such as the bottom of a small plastic deli container or margarine tub, with moistened sand. Place it in the tank and cover it with a much larger shelter, either plastic or clay. The inside of the shelter will then consist of an outer dry area and a central damp area. With this type of shelter, fat-tailed geckos will be able to select the level of substrate moisture and the air humidity inside the shelter will be raised. Females will typically lay eggs in the moist sand containers.

African fat-tailed geckos require higher relative air humidity than do leopard geckos; mist two to three times a week.

Heating
The best systems for heating fat-tailed gecko cages are heat tapes or reptile heating pads that create temperature gradients of 82–90° F within the cage. The animals should be maintained at cooler temperatures, 68–72° F, for prebreeding conditioning.

The starburst fat-tailed gecko is a morph with reduced banding that was developed by Mark Leshock.

The African fat-tailed gecko (*Hemitheconyx caudicinctus*) is another popular gecko.

Maintenance

Shelter maintenance is the same as with leopard geckos except the cages of adults should be misted twice a week. Lightly mist juveniles once daily.

Feeding

Feed fat-tailed geckos as you would leopard geckos except offer your fat-tailed geckos newborn to one-week-old mice with their rumps dipped in calcium at least once every two weeks. An increased percentage of pink mice in the diet can help improve reproductive success.

Clean water should be available at all times.

Breeding

African fat-tailed geckos are generally more difficult to breed than leopard geckos. Often, females in captivity will lay several clutches of infertile eggs. Other common problems include the embryo dying before reaching full term or failing to break out of the egg.

For successful breeding of fat-tailed geckos, there are several things you should do.
- Select only healthy animals with significant fat reserves for breeding.
- Keep individual sexes separately.
- Cool down males and females starting in October or November for two months. Allow the ambient temper-

ature to drop to 68–72° F while keeping the heat cable or strip on the low setting. If a heating pad is used, move it so that only a small strip is underneath the enclosure and keep at a lower setting. During the cooling period, don't offer the animals food. Provide water but do not mist.

- After the two-month cooling period, place the animals back on a regular maintenance schedule. Offer food to females more frequently (every other day). Once a week, feed the geckos pink mice with the rumps dipped in calcium.

- Two to three weeks after the animals are back on a normal schedule, introduce a female to a cage containing a single male for one day, once a week, for three weeks. Remove the females after observing successful copulation. It is a good idea to have more than one male for breeding because all males are not equally fertile.

- During the breeding season, which can last several months, females can produce two to seven clutches of two eggs each. If introduced to a male within a day or two of egg-laying, copulation will often follow. Females must be closely monitored during breeding. Take care to provide optimal maintenance, feeding, and watering.

African fat-tailed geckos are the rising stars of "geckodom" with beautiful new morphs that have captured the interests of hobbyists.

Care of Eggs

Offer your African fat-tailed gecko a covered container with moistened vermiculite or sand in which to lay its eggs. A hole should be cut out of the side of the container for the gravid female to enter the shelter. The shelter should have a moist medium. Unfortunately, fat-tailed geckos often bury their eggs in some other area of the enclosure; sometimes right near the heat source. It is important that during the breeding season you check the gravid female's enclosure at least twice a day. Fat-tailed gecko eggs can dehydrate rapidly and many breeders lose eggs because they fail to inspect the enclosure frequently enough. Keep on top of the situation.

Incubation of Eggs

Incubate fat-tailed gecko eggs in the same manner and at the same temperature as leopard gecko eggs. The recommended incubation temperature is 85° F. As with leopard geckos, incubation temperature plays a significant role in sex determination. At a temperature of 88–90° F, you can expect a greater ratio of males.

For African fat-tailed geckos, the incubation period ranges from 39½ days at 93° F to 72½ days at 82.4° F. African fat-tailed geckos cannot tolerate the lower incubation temperatures that their more temperate relative, the leopard gecko, can. This may explain why many breeders have had difficulty with this species. The viable range of incubation temperatures for African fat-tailed geckos is from 82.4° F to over 97° F.

Pictured is a baby white-striped African fat-tailed gecko.

Raising Juveniles

Hatchling fat-tailed geckos are typically smaller and more delicate than hatchling leopard geckos. They should be housed individually in plastic shoeboxes and kept on either paper towel or fine-grade orchid bark. Hatchling geckos will not feed until after their first shed (three to four days after hatching). During this interim period, keep them warm and provide water in a shallow dish at all times. Mist the enclosure lightly once daily to maintain adequate relative air humidity. Provide a small shelter.

After shedding, most hatchlings will feed readily on three-week old crickets coated with a vitamin/mineral supplement. The feeding schedule should be the same as for baby leopard geckos. Take care not to introduce too many crickets or large oversized crickets—this can traumatize the baby lizards. Initially, offer only two- to three-week-old (¼ inch) crickets. Hatchling fat-tailed geckos are shy, reclusive little creatures. Some babies may not begin feeding after their first shed. Hand-feed reluctant babies or they may start to decline.

CHAPTER 14
OTHER EUBLEPHARIDS

African Clawed Gecko (*Holodactylus africanus*)

S mall numbers of this species have been imported in recent years from Tanzania. In the wild, they are commonly found in sandy washes. This is a small eublepharid with very large eyes that digs burrows. The majority of imported animals are males—easily recognized by their hemipenal bulges. Many clawed geckos come in stressed and dehydrated, but most will acclimate as long as basic protocols are followed. These odd little creatures are best left to specialists.

The African clawed gecko (*Holodactylus africanus*) is best left to experts.

Distribution
Somalia south to Tanzania.

Size
Up to 4 inches long.

Care
They should be kept on several inches of sand/soil mix with a little clay to prevent burrows from collapsing. A

couple of days before introducing geckos, add water to the mix, pat it down, and allow the top layers to dry out. This will add cohesion to the burrows. Water should be added weekly at one end of the vivarium so that the bottom 25 percent of the substrate is moistened. An alternative is to keep these geckos on a thinner layer of substrate and offer a humidified shelter.

One-third of the floor of the enclosure should be heated with a sub-tank heating pad. No special lighting is required as these lizards will spend the day concealed. As with fat-tailed geckos, they will readily feed on two- to three-week-old supplemented crickets. This species has been bred and hatched in the United States, but the primary difficulty is obtaining females.

Japanese Leopard Gecko *(Goniurosaurus kuroiwae splendens)*

This is one of the most rare eublepharids and only small numbers are in U.S. collections. The native name is *Tokage Modoki*. They are not found on the Japanese mainland but on several of the many islands that make up the Ryukyu Archipelago.

The Japanese leopard gecko *(Goniurosaurus kuroiwae splendens)* should not be handled.

Distribution
Islands of the Ryukyu Archipelago, Japan.

Size
Up to 6 inches long.

Care

They do best if kept in the upper 70s F and will tolerate night drops into the 60s F. Slight winter cooling is recommended for breeding success. Three to four clutches of eggs are laid per year; they hatch in two to two and half months if kept at 78–80° F. These geckos have been successfully maintained in tall, plastic storage containers or they can be kept on orchid bark with an area of moistened green moss and cork bark sections for shelter. Lightly mist the enclosure once or twice daily. In dry areas, cover half of the screen top or use a cool-air humidifier in the room. Angle large cork bark sections across the tank for climbing. As with all eublepharids, keep only one male per container with one or more females.

In recent years, two large undescribed species of *Goniurosaurus* with red-orange irises have been imported, one from north Vietnam and the other from southern China. Their care is similar to that of the Japanese leopard gecko. All species of *Goniurosaurus* are easily stressed and should not be handled except for maintenance purposes.

Malaysian Cat Gecko (*Aeluroscalabotes felinus*)

This is the most unique of the eublepharids. It is semiarboreal and has opposable digits, allowing it to climb on

The Malaysian cat gecko *(Aeluroscalabotes felinus)* should become increasingly available.

vegetation. It has been placed in its own subfamily, the Aeluroscalabotinae. Few specimens have been imported and of those even fewer have acclimated to captivity.

Distribution
Thailand, south through peninsular Malaysia and Borneo.

Size
Up to 7 inches long.

Care
Because they are easily stressed, these geckos are usually kept singly except during breeding when a male is introduced to a female's enclosure. The cat gecko requires high relative humidity; it is best to keep them in covered plastic storage containers (sweater-box size or larger) with holes punched in the side for ventilation. The substrate should be potting soil with an area of moistened green moss. Provide a shelter, climbing branches, and a shallow water dish. Lightly mist once in the evening. This species does best at moderate temperatures but should be kept slightly cooler and drier for up to eight weeks for prebreeding conditioning. High humidity will stimulate breeding, so raise temperatures and mist more frequently. Fortunately, a few specialists have had success breeding this species, so it may become more readily available in the future.

Central American Banded Gecko (Coleonyx mitratus)
This Central American gecko is occasionally imported and is bred in some numbers by hobbyists. Imports may

The Central American banded gecko (Coleonyx mitratus) is easily kept in captivity.

require veterinary treatment for parasites, but once established, this is a hardy and easily maintained species.

Distribution
From Guatemala to Costa Rica.

Size
6 inches long.

Care
Central American banded geckos can easily be kept in plastic storage boxes, or vivaria with a peat sand mix or small orchid bark as substrate. Provide an area of moistened green moss. Provide a shelter and mist the enclosure once a day in the evening.

Central American banded geckos fare well on supplemented three-week old crickets. Keep at temperatures between 74–82° F.

Banded geckos are very prolific in captivity, laying up to eleven clutches a year. Eggs can be incubated like leopard gecko eggs at 78–82° F. The young are very attractive—velvety brown with high-contrast, pale-yellow bands. This species is nervous and does not tolerate handling well. A related species, the Yucatan banded gecko *(Coleonyx elegans)*, is sometimes available for purchase. According to one private herpetoculturist, David Perlowin, its care is similar to the Central American banded gecko's, except that is has a low tolerance for dietary vitamin D_3. This may account for the failure of herpetoculturists to establish this beautiful species, and for the high mortality at all stages from embryos and hatchlings to adults.

Tucson Banded Gecko *(Coleonyx variegatus bogerti)* and Texas Banded Gecko *(Coleonyx brevis)*

Their small size and protection from commercial collection over most of their range means these geckos are seldom available and of little interest to breeders. However, this group deserves more attention from herpetoculturists.

The Tucson banded gecko *(Coleonyx variegatus bogerti)* is endemic to North America.

Several species are attractive and are ideal for those interested in keeping smaller lizards.

Care

Banded geckos are small, desert-dwelling eublepharids that can be maintained like leopard geckos except that they should be offered small crickets (⅛ inch to ¼ inch) as their primary diet. Selective breeding, as with leopard geckos, could result in beautiful morphs. They should be cooled and exposed to a shorter photoperiod during the winter for successful breeding.

The Texas banded gecko *(Coleonyx brevis)* is quite similar to its Arizona cousin.

REFERENCES

Allen, R. 1987. Captive care and breeding of the leopard gecko, *Eublepharis macularius. Reptiles: Proceedings of the 1986 U.K. Herpetological Societies' Symposium on Captive Breeding.* 27–30.

Anderson, A., and C. Oldham. 1986. Captive husbandry and propagation of the African fat-tail gecko, *Hemitheconyx caudicinctus. Proceedings of the 10th International Herpetological Symposium on Captive Propagation and Husbandry.* 75–85.

Autum, K., and D.F. De Nardo. 1995. Thermoregulation and growth rates in leopard geckos. *Journal of Herpetology.* 29:157–162.

Bull, J.J. 1987. Temperature-dependent sex determination in reptiles: validity of sex diagnosis in hatchling lizards. *Can. J. Zool.* 65:1421–1424.

Bull, J.J. 1980. Sex determination in reptiles. Q. *Rev Biol.* 55: 2–21.

DiPrima, A.M., B.E. Viets, and C.F. Williams. 1997. The effects of sex, incubation temperature, and heritability on pigmentation in the leopard gecko, *Eublepharis macularius. 77th Annual Meeting of the American Society of Ichthyologists and Herpetologists.*

Gamble, T. 1997. *A Leopard Gecko Bibliography.* 30pp, self published. *This is an important reference on the bibliography of leopard gecko and invaluable for any one doing research on this species.*

Grismer. L. I. 1997. Eublepharid Geckos. Living Relics of Gekkotan Evolution. *Fauna.*1:1. *A fine overview of eublepharid geckos illustrated with many color photographs.*

Grismer, L.I. 1988. Phylogeny, taxonomy, classification, and biogeography of eublepharid geckos. In R. Estes and G. Pregill, eds. *Phylogenetic Relationships of the Lizard Families.* Stanford, Calif.: 369-469. Stanford University Press. *The most current view on the phylogeny and taxonomy of eublepharids and a good introduction to the methodology of herpetology.*

Gutzke, W.H.N., and D. Crews. 1988. Embryonic temperature determines adult sexuality in a reptile. *Nature.* 332: 832–834.

Heidemann, R.L., and B.E. Viets. 1995. The effects of incubation temperature on sex and growth in the gecko, *Hemitheconyx caudicinctus. 75th Annual Meeting of the American Society of Ichthyologists and Herpetologists.*

Heidemann, R.L., and B.E. Viets. 1996. The effect of male body size on dominance and mate acquisition in the gecko, *Hemitheconyx caudicinctus. 39th Annual Meeting of the Society for the Study of Amphibians and Reptiles.*

Lui.W. 1996. Captive Husbandry and Breeding of the Malaysian Cat Gecko., *Aeluroscalabotes felinus. International Reptilian. 4: 3.*

Nunan, J. 1987. Prevention of dehydration and calcium depletion in deserticolous geckos. *Captive Propagation and Husbandry of Reptiles and Amphibians.* Northern California Herpetological Society. 4: 43–47.

Slavens, F. and K. Slavens. 1997. *Reptiles and Amphibians in Captivity: Breeding, Longevity and Inventory.* Seattle, Wash.: Slaveware.

Thorogood, J., and I.W. Whimster. 1979. The maintenance and breeding of the leopard gecko, *Eublepharis macularius,* as a laboratory animal. *International Zoo Yearbook.* 19: 74–78.

Tousignant, A., B. Viets, D. Flores, and D. Crews. 1995. Ontogenetic and social factors affect the endocrinology and timing of reproduction in the female leopard gecko, *Eublepharis macularius. Hormones and Behavior.* 29:141–153.

Viets, B.E., M.A. Ewert, L.G. Talent, and C.E. Nelson. 1994. Sex-determining mechanisms in squamate reptiles. *The Journal of Experimental Zoology.* 270: 45–56.

Viets, B.E., A. Tousignant, M.A. Ewert, C.E. Nelson, and D. Crews. 1993. Temperature-dependent sex determination in the leopard gecko, *Eublepharis macularius. The Journal of Experimental Zoology.* 265: 679–683.

Wagner, E. 1974. Breeding of the leopard gecko, *Eublepharis macularius,* at the Seattle Zoo. *International Zoo Yearbook.* 14: 84–86.

Wise, S. 1994. An analysis of behavioral interactions in the leopard gecko, *Eublepharis macularius. One hundred and fourth Annual Meeting of the Nebraska Academy of Sciences.*

Yaverkin, Y. I. and N. L. Orlov. 1998. Captive Breeding of Cat Geckos. *Dactylus.* 3:3, 87–89.

INDEX

ABOUT THE AUTHOR

Philippe de Vosjoli is the highly acclaimed author of the best-selling reptile-care books, The Herpetocultural Library Series. His work in the field of herpetoculture has been recognized nationally and internationally for establishing high standards for amphibian and reptile care. His books, articles, and other writings have been praised and recommended by numerous herpetological societies, veterinarians, and other experts in the field. Philippe de Vosjoli was also the cofounder and president of The American Federation of Herpetoculturists, and was given the Josef Laszlo Memorial Award in 1995 for excellence in herpetoculture and his contribution to the advancement of the field.